21st Century Architecture
ALFRESCO *Living*

Edited

images
Publishing

ALFRESCO *Living*

21st Century Architecture

ALFRESCO *Living*

Edited by Mandy Herbet

images
Publishing

Published in Australia in 2013 by

The Images Publishing Group Pty Ltd

ABN 89 059 734 431

6 Bastow Place, Mulgrave, Victoria 3170, Australia

Tel: +61 3 9561 5544 Fax: +61 3 9561 4860

books@imagespublishing.com

www.imagespublishing.com

National Library of Australia Cataloguing-in-Publication entry

Title:	Alfresco living / edited by Mandy Herbet.
ISBN:	978 1 86470 512 6 (hbk.)
Series:	21st century architecture
Notes:	Includes index.
Subjects:	Outdoor living spaces.
	Architecture, Domestic – 21st century.
Other Authors/Contributors:	Herbet, Mandy.
Dewey Number:	721.84

Edited by Mandy Herbet

Designed by The Graphic Image Studio Pty Ltd, Mulgrave, Australia
www.tgis.com.au

Pre-publishing services by United Graphic Pte Ltd, Singapore
Printed on 140gsm GoldEast Matt Art by 1010 Printing International Limited in China

IMAGES has included on its website a page for special notices in relation to this and our
other publications. Please visit www.imagespublishing.com.

Contents

Introduction

Mandy Herbet

Editor

Courtyards and outdoor living spaces have been part of residential life as long as people have lived in enclosed spaces. The earliest known courtyard houses are known to date back to 3000 B.C. and while courtyards are more prevalent in tropical climates, the comforts of light, privacy and tranquility offered by alfresco living areas are universal.

Alfresco living is not simply about the designated areas we associate with being outside – the courtyards, the decks, the swimming pools. It's about opening up to bring the outside inside thereby creating an unrestricted living space. There's a sense of freedom to alfresco living – letting go of the constraints of the everyday and embracing the bonhomie of having friends and family around. But a great outdoor space can also lend itself to solitary reflection – a quiet sense of space, where time is elastic. The homes featured in this book range from the expansive ranch home in Nevada to a tucked-away rooftop garden in the middle of New York; from a tropical wonderland in Singapore to a quiet heritage home in Melbourne; but they all incorporate the environment surrounding them into a welcoming alfresco living space.

With all the demands of our modern world, having an outdoor living space to enjoy seems to be more important than ever. In *Bahia House*, the traditional Bahia-style home has been updated for the 21st century while retaining all the ecological features that work so well in that climate. Found in the deserts of Arizona, *The Six* features those same important features to enhance ventilation and livable space. The central courtyard also creates a shared living area and a sense of community, which quietly enhances daily life.

Alfresco living isn't restricted by the amount of space available. Despite space being at a premium in the high-density neighbourhoods of Japan, the internal courtyard in *Skycatcher House* helps create a meditative space, while the Los Angeles home, *Oriole Way Residence*, uses city views to create a sense of personal space in the claustrophobic city scene.

Conversely, some projects have expansive sites available to them and the architects have found ways to use the space in such a way that there is still a sense of intimacy. In *Story Pool Pavilion*, the architects used an already well-loved plateau to create an outdoor area built around the existing Airstream trailer, balancing the generous views with intimate shaded spaces and a sense of the client's personality. In *SGNW House*, which is part of the lush Zimbali Coastal Resort in South Africa, the outside is woven throughout the house, with courtyards and Koi ponds visible from wherever you find yourself. This is truly alfresco living at its most luxurious.

These are simply a selection of the fantastic projects we have to share with you in *Alfresco Living*. Each project highlights a different aspect of the architecture contained in this type of lifestyle and different challenges faced by the architects in creating these spaces. I hope you'll be as excited paging through this book as I was when editing it.

Appleton Living

California, USA

Minarc

Oriented to ensure that all the rooms have access to the outdoor living area, which includes a pool, outdoor dining, barbecue and play court, Appleton Living is also designed to maximise passive solar gain and natural ventilation.

The solar chimney for releasing hot air during the summer and heating cold air during the winter eliminated the need for mechanical air handling. The design elements are oriented to take optimum advantage of natural light and cross ventilation to cut down electrical costs.

The interior and exterior courtyards allow for natural ventilation, as do the master sliding window and living room sliders. Solar thermal radiant floor heating exists throughout the house while a heated patio and fireplace for outdoor dining maximises indoor/outdoor living. The entry living room has glass to both sides to further connect the interior spaces to the outdoor living areas. Floor and ceiling materials connect in an unobtrusive and whimsical manner to increase floor plan flow and space.

Magnetic chalkboard sliders in the play area and paperboard sliders in the kids' rooms transform the house itself into a medium for childhood artistic expression. The simple eco-conscious design is focused on functionality and creating a healthy family environment. There is a conscious effort to only use materials in their most organic form and the contrasts between the stone, steel and wood help to make this modern home warm and family-friendly.

Photography by Art Gray

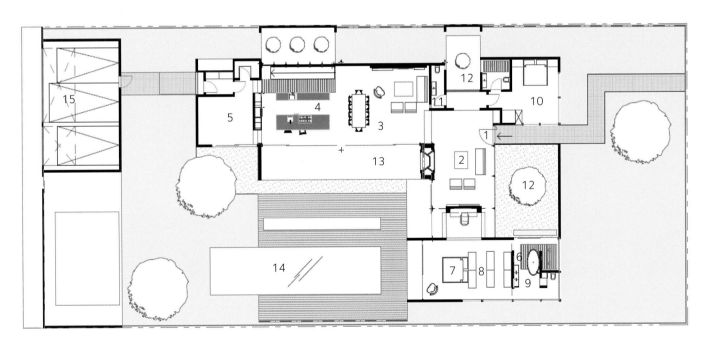

1	Entry	6	Office	11	Powder room
2	Living	7	Master bedroom	12	Courtyard
3	Dining	8	Master closet	13	Verandah
4	Kitchen	9	Master bathroom	14	Pool
5	TV/play room	10	Guest suite	15	Garage

Armitage
Residence

Melbourne, Australia

Centrum Architects + Jack Merlo Landscape Design and Construction

Challenged by the increasing needs of a growing family and wanting to stay in the established neighbourhood that they had come to love, the clients asked Ken Charles of Centrum Architects to maximise all opportunities their existing house and site had to offer – inherent in this was the need to maintain courtyard spaces as places for specific activities as well as extending the visual and functional areas of the house itself. They also wanted to provide private spaces for all family members to withdraw to at times but to balance these with large interconnected communal spaces, both internal and external, allowing for the family to grow.

To meet this challenge Centrum Architects located the home theatre room and cellar in a basement under the new garage and opened the garage directly onto the lane. The space previously taken up with driveways could then be reworked to significantly increase the amenity of the ground floor areas.

The courtyards are very much integral to the design of the house. The pool courtyard on the eastern side provides an intense activity zone for the summer. Large windows from the bedroom and sitting room enjoy a relaxing aspect onto the water at other times and particularly at night with floodlighting on.

The entertaining courtyard to the rear is accessed from the main living and dining areas and large retractable glass and steel multifold doors enable all these spaces to be fused into one large plaza, which could be used for a variety of family activities as well as parties and entertaining. By incorporating all the main family spaces in a U-shape around much of the entertaining courtyard, visual connection is maintained between family members in different parts of the family space rather than being isolated with their activities in separate rooms.

Landscape architect Jack Merlo also worked closely with the family to ensure the courtyard detail further enhanced the design opportunities. The barbecue and external fireplace become year round facilities and the large projecting steel beams provide support for retractable sunshading on hot days. The colour palette for the interior spills out to the external spaces and careful plant selection further enhances the textures from the mostly natural materials in the construction.

Photography by Mark Fergus Photography

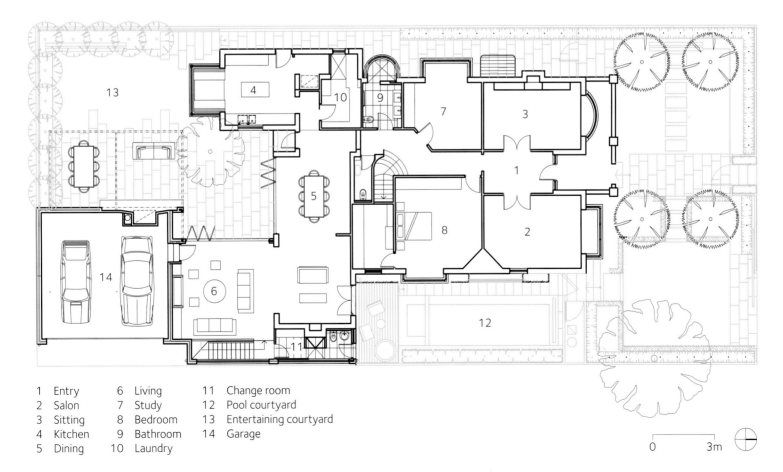

1	Entry	6	Living	11	Change room
2	Salon	7	Study	12	Pool courtyard
3	Sitting	8	Bedroom	13	Entertaining courtyard
4	Kitchen	9	Bathroom	14	Garage
5	Dining	10	Laundry		

0   3m

Bahia House

Salvador, Brazil

Studio mk27 – Marcio Kogan and Suzana Glogowski

The Bahia House is an ecological house but not in the technological sense; not in the contemporary sense of the word 'sustainability'. It does not have the very latest state-of-the-art gadgets that make it possible to optimise electric expenditure. The organisation of the floor plan and the use of materials come close to those of traditional architecture, with the Bahia House making use of the old popular knowledge that has been reinvented and incorporated throughout the history of Brazilian architecture. In building the house, architects Marcio Kogan and Suzana Glogowski from Studio mk27 considered the location and the climate and designed a 'green' house using traditional Bahian designs.

The builders of Bahian traditional houses have long known how to keep interiors cool even in blazing temperatures of more than 40°C. These houses have roofs of clay and wooden ceilings. The openings have large panels of wooden Mashrabiyas brought to Brazil by the Portuguese colonial architecture since the first centuries of its occupation of the American territories, and its origin is of an Arabian cultural influence. These wooden panels provide vast comfort to the interior. The traditional Bahian house uses the north-eastern wind blowing in from the sea to organise the floor plan and has cross ventilation in its principal spaces, always making the interior cool and airy.

The Bahia House uses all these elements. Adjusting the Portuguese house to the tropical climate has resulted in a very pleasant house, where the interior is protected from the outside heat.

The floor plan is entirely organised around a central patio, making cross ventilation in all the spaces possible and a view that looks in to a grassed garden and two mango trees. The Bahia House privileges the environmental comfort of its dwellers but does not make use of the most modern technology in order to achieve this comfort.

Photography by Nelson Kon

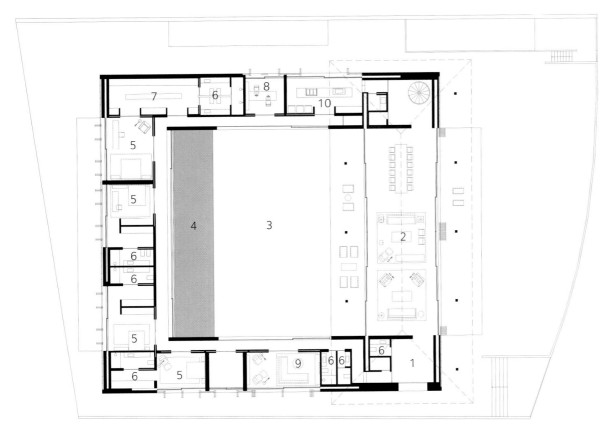

1   Entry
2   Living room
3   Patio
4   Reflective pool
5   Bedroom
6   Bathroom
7   Closet
8   Home office
9   Gym
10 Kitchen

0   5m

Basser
House

Melbourne, Australia

Mihaly Slocombe

Basser House is a renovation for a small family to an existing single-storey, double-fronted, red brick dwelling built in 1902 in the Edwardian style. The house is located in one of the oldest, most established suburbs of Melbourne. The brief was to straighten out the cramped living areas of the original house to accommodate large dinner parties while retaining a sense of intimacy when occupied by our clients alone. The addition was to make the most of a tight site and provide a stronger link to the under-utilised back garden.

Architects Mihaly Slocombe's design response seeks a thorough and intimate dialogue between the existing and new parts of the dwelling – the form, planning arrangement and details of the addition learn from characteristics of the original house, but improve upon them. Within this dialogue, the environmental parameters of the site are addressed via simple passive solar techniques that cost little but achieve a lot. A colour palette is substituted for one of texture – paint, glass, wallpaper, marble and laminate are combined in shades of white that create a richly tactile experience. The roofs and sculpted ceilings of the addition reveal these ideas in a holistic and exuberant way, honouring the qualities of the original house, permitting direct sunlight into, and natural ventilation through, the living spaces, and celebrating the activities taking place beneath.

Basser House is a study in rational planning, reflecting upon the layout of the double-fronted housing typology with its central corridor and discrete spaces either side. The central corridor continues into the extension as a timber-clad 'runway' that opens up on both sides to establish a freedom of movement between the kitchen, living and dining areas and the courtyard. The presence of this corridor is marked only by a change in flooring material, from the timber of the existing to the concrete of the new. This grafting of the addition onto the existing dwelling is done in such a way that the new references the old with a spark of originality. The palette of textures used includes paint, marble, laminate and wallpaper, and they all work together to reflect the client's personality.

Photography by Peter Bennetts

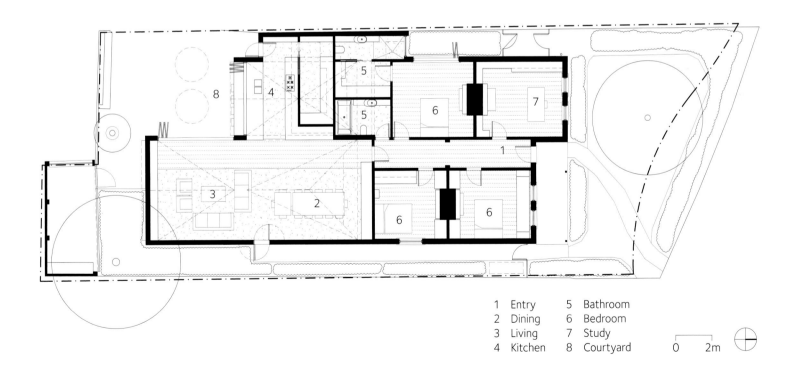

1	Entry	5	Bathroom
2	Dining	6	Bedroom
3	Living	7	Study
4	Kitchen	8	Courtyard

0   2m

Berkshire Residence

Texas, USA

Morrison Dilworth + Walls

The design of this home began with the site. Morrison Dilworth + Walls' goals were to take advantage of the site's best feature – the mature trees in the front of the property – and to mitigate the negative aspect of the traffic noise on a busy thoroughfare at the rear of the property.

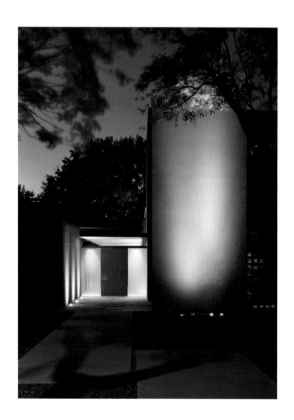

This strategy led to the U-shaped plan that forms a courtyard toward the front, facing the trees, and simultaneously uses the mass of the house to block the noise from the highway behind. The less inhabited space at the rear of the site is being developed as a sculpture garden.

The owners have a large extended family and entertain frequently so the house opens to the courtyard and swimming pool on all sides. Large glass doors slide into pockets in the exterior walls thereby creating an environment where outside and inside become one.

The disposition and scale of the rooms surrounding the courtyard make the house ideal for a range of uses, from one or two people enjoying the space, to entertaining on a large scale.

The exterior of the house is rendered in dark, grey-green stucco that allows the house to blend into its wooded site and reside comfortably within the surrounding neighbourhood. Teak screens are strategically inserted into the exterior walls. In addition to their functional purpose, the screens recall the material used in the making of the outdoor line of furniture created and sold by the owners.

Photography by Charles Davis Smith, AIA

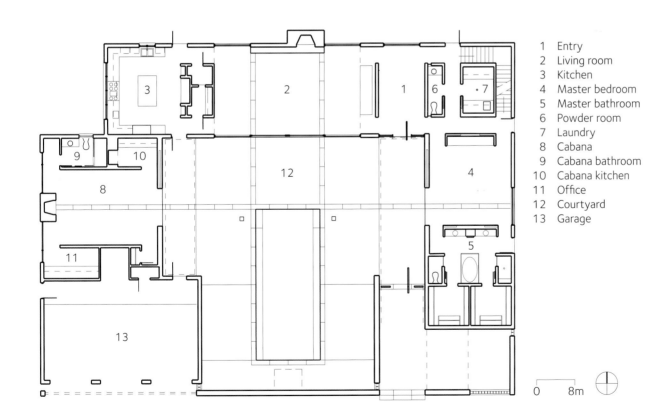

1   Entry
2   Living room
3   Kitchen
4   Master bedroom
5   Master bathroom
6   Powder room
7   Laundry
8   Cabana
9   Cabana bathroom
10 Cabana kitchen
11 Office
12 Courtyard
13 Garage

0   8m

Birchgrove House

Sydney, Australia

Pearse Architects with Brian Keirnan

An extension and renovation to an existing house, the relationship to the garden was central to the design. This relationship is a spatial connection – you cannot walk directly from one to the other – it only feels like you are connected; this was a way of resolving the 750-millimetre (30-inch) height difference from the floor to garden levels.

Because of this variation in height, Pearse Architects, in collaboration with Brian Keirnan, felt an intermediate element was needed and settled on a pond due to the special quality water has in a garden: its ever-changing colours and reflections; the way it feels like a step but isn't one; and the way it could slide back under the family room floor.

The design pushes the house up to a clump of mature palm trees, and uses them as a separating device. Keeping them was also symbolic as planting them was one of the first acts of the new owners when they bought the land many years ago.

The interiors also needed shielding from overlooking on one side, while keeping the house open to the garden. Stepping joinery units plus the wide roof cantilever at the entrance porch work as privacy screens; and views of the garden are still available between and around the joinery.

From the garden the strong horizontality of the house dramatises the relative height of the low house compared to the relatively tall garden and the exposed steel roof edge beams balances the strong vertical lines of the palm tree trunks.

Photography by Steve Back

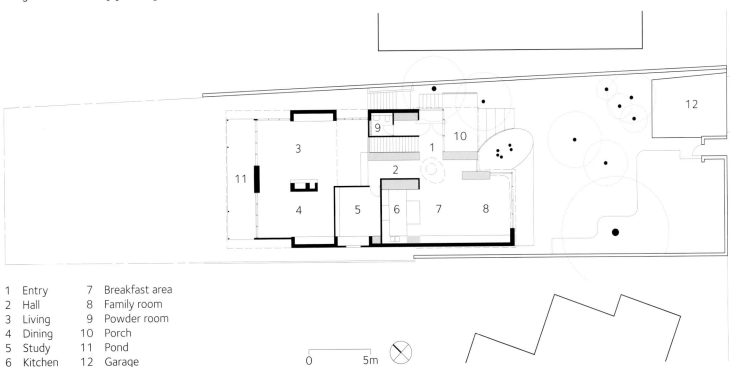

1	Entry	7	Breakfast area
2	Hall	8	Family room
3	Living	9	Powder room
4	Dining	10	Porch
5	Study	11	Pond
6	Kitchen	12	Garage

0   5m

Bronte
House

Sydney, Australia

Rolf Ockert Design

The client approached Rolf Ockert Design to create the house of their dreams on a site perched high over the Pacific Ocean; a home that was to make them feel like being on holiday every day. While the view was fantastic, the site was very small and suffocated by overbearing neighbouring dwellings.

The finished house feels generous, as if it is alone with the ocean and the sky. High side walls offer a sense of privacy but also provide mass for a comfortable indoor climate and have continuous highlight windows for the enjoyment of 360-degree views of the sky. The large face concrete wall dominating the space has slim slot windows, allowing teasing glimpses of the ocean when entering the house while effectively cutting out the visual presence of neighbouring properties.

The house opens itself up completely to the east, which presents stunning water views. This also allows the house to capture the constant ocean breezes to cool down throughout the year. These breezes are easily regulated by a plethora of ventilation options from sliding doors to operable louvres.

A rich but reduced palette of strong, earthy materials – from concrete to timber flooring and ceilings, rust metal finishes and thick, textured renders – contrasts with the fine detailing of the interior and anchors the residence against the airy, light aspect created by the opening to the views.

Photography by client

FIRST FLOOR

1 Entry
2 Rumpus room
3 Master bedroom
4 Master bathroom
5 Closet
6 WC/Laundry
7 Dining
8 Kitchen
9 Living
10 Formal dining
11 Study
12 Bedroom
13 Bathroom
14 WC
15 Deck
16 Pool
17 Carport

GROUND FLOOR

0   5m

Casa Joya

San Miguel de Allende, Mexico

House + House Architects

At the end of a narrow pedestrian lane in the historic centre of San Miguel de Allende, Mexico this home sits comfortably on a small 10-metre-by-10-metre (33-foot-by-33 foot) lot. Dimensions guided every design decision in order to fit living, dining, kitchen, family, three bedrooms, two bathrooms, powder, and a courtyard, terraces and balconies onto this tiny piece of land. A 10-metre (33-foot) cube became the ideal size for this jewel box – Casa Joya. Curving walls of glass and plaster link each space to the outdoors, swept with shimmers of sunlight that change throughout the day. A triangular spiral stairway spins movement up to the roof terrace with views to luminous sunsets and myriad church towers.

Walls washed with naturally pigmented lime glow soft and warm under sunlight pouring in through the skylight above the stairway. Spaces borrow from each other, layering together in the illusion of a grander volume. Six-metre-high (20-foot) ceilings in the living room with a 5.5-metre-high (18-foot) wall of gridded glass belie any sense that this is a small home. Folding glass doors allow inside and outside to flow together in this comfortable climate. A two-storey-high stone fountain and water-wall send ripples of light and sound throughout the home to complement the sounds of roosters, church bells and calls from wandering vendors.

Black cantera stone floors are locally quarried and the swirling stone pattern in the courtyard paving symbolises the life path of the homeowners. Windows, doors and whimsical steel railings were handmade by the local blacksmith, the flaming sculpture in the fireplace assembled by the plumber and the gridded entry door, cabinets and dining table that unfolds to seat 10 fabricated by the carpenter in his open air workshop. There is a sense of sanctuary in the airy glow of this dream at the end of the homeowners' long journey to this special place. The craftsmen who built this home are men who bring a spiritual joy to their work, imbuing this unique place with an aura of magic.

Photography by Steven and Cathi House

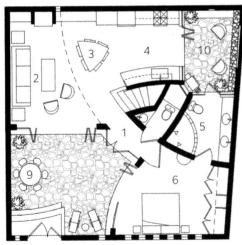

GROUND FLOOR

FIRST FLOOR

SECOND FLOOR

0   2m

1	Entry	5	Bathroom	9 Porch
2	Living room	6	Master bedroom	10 Garden terrace
3	Dining room	7	Bedroom	11 Terrace
4	Kitchen	8	Family room	

Casa Panamá

São Paulo, Brazil

Studio mk27 – Marcio Kogan
+ Samanta Cafardo

Casa Panamá is located in a garden neighbourhood just a few blocks
from Paulista, the financial centre of the city of São Paulo. The
owner has an important art collection that comprises, above all,
modern Brazilian art, and the house and gardens were designed to
accommodate this collection. Works of art are scattered throughout
all areas of the residence, from the bedrooms to the various courtyard
gardens and terraces.

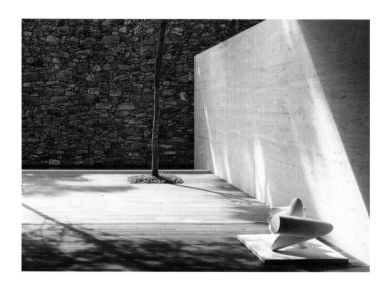

The interior plan is organised across three floors and a subsolo, or underground level. Upon entering the lot, a tree-covered patio leads to the front door. A social hall distributes part of the program of the house: a library, vertical circulation, the utility rooms and the living room. From within the library a sculpture by Maria Martins can be seen in front of the exterior stone wall, reposing over a reflecting pool. The living room features large movable wall spans that open in their entirety to the main courtyard garden, building a visually impressive spatial continuity between interior and exterior. In the garden, a pool installed on the side of the lot mirrors the stones of the wall.

On the second floor, a large corridor connecting the bedrooms also works as a gallery exhibiting paintings and sculptures. An office annexed to the master suite overlooks the garden, as do the other bedrooms, their façades featuring brise-soleils made of sliding vertical wooden lathes. One of the architectural premises of the house was to organise the space around a wooden box that is placed inside a C-shaped concrete cask. This concrete cask is formed by cement slabs and a wall, and determines the translucent and transparent areas in relation to the wooden box. On the third storey, a games room and a gym connect to a wooden deck, the terrace of the house. The utility rooms of the house and the garage are located on the basement level.

Stone and the wood, materials that refer to traditional Brazilian building, are mixed with modern materials, such as reinforced concrete and plastic, to create a distinct architectural language.

Photography by Nelson Kon

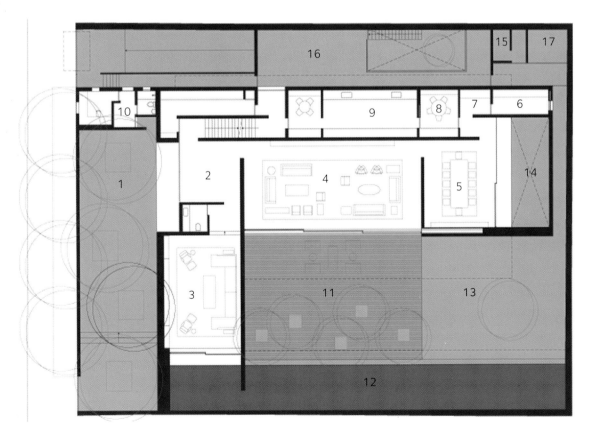

1 Entry
2 Hall
3 Library
4 Living room
5 Dining room
6 China closet
7 Wine storage
8 Lunch room
9 Kitchen
10 Sentry box
11 Deck
12 Swimming pool
13 Garden
14 Courtyard
15 Dog house
16 Service patio

0   6m

Cluny
House

Singapore

Guz Architects

The Cluny House in Singapore demonstrates how technology, planning and design can be applied sensitively to generate a comfortable, luxurious, yet sustainable family home. This 'green' project by Guz Architects employs photovoltaic cells and solar water heaters together with design for passive cooling and cross ventilation, which helps to reduce energy usage. Irrigation tanks and roof gardens collect and recycle rainwater; and the use of materials such as recycled teak and artificial timber adds warmth without compromising the finite resources of our environment.

The home's living space is laid out around a central water court, forming the focal point of the project. Lushly planted roof gardens surround this courtyard and greenery can be seen from every room, adding to the effect of nature surrounding and enveloping the house.

The high-tech elements of the house include state of the art EIB systems, photovoltaic cells and security systems integrated discreetly and working with the natural environment of the house rather than against it. This integration of technology and nature deserves special mention in a compelling design that could realistically become the model for sustainable living.

Photography by Patrick Bingham-Hall

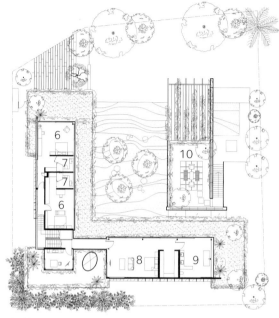

FIRST FLOOR

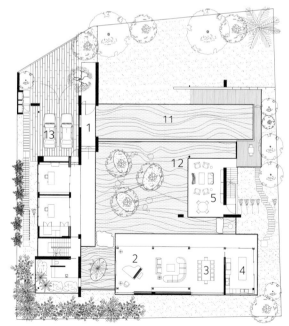

GROUND FLOOR

1   Entry
2   Living
3   Dining
4   Kitchen
5   Covered terrace
6   Bedroom
7   Bathroom
8   Master bedroom
9   Master bathroom
10 Rooftop patio
11 Pool
12 Pond
13 Garage

0   4m

Coleman Residence

City Beach, Australia

iredale pedersen hook

The Coleman Residence explores the illusion of the home as a holiday retreat, exploiting the tapering boundaries with a vanishing point that meets in the neighbouring property. It engages with the possibility of spatial illusion resulting from the perspective approach to spatial construction and the relationship of the everyday experience of the family residence. The vanishing point is denied visibility by a wall at the end of the property that serves to exaggerate the illusion with an installation by the artist Jurek Wybraniec.

Analogous to a wedge of Camembert cheese, the tactile and sensuous materials are reserved for the interior spaces and courtyards. The large, anonymous, external white walls resonate as powerful barriers, carefully concealing the internal richness of the private world.

All space is organised as a series of wedges that connect to the illusory vanishing point. These wedges collect interior and exterior space. Driving through the middle of the residence is a wedge of

recycled Jarrah, a large deck that starts at the street boundary and ends 1.5 metres (5 feet) back from the rear boundary. This wedge connects the interior and exterior, forming spaces of ambiguity and creating a resonating curved court that brings the exterior deep in to the interior.

Photography by Patrick Bingham-Hall and Peter Bennetts

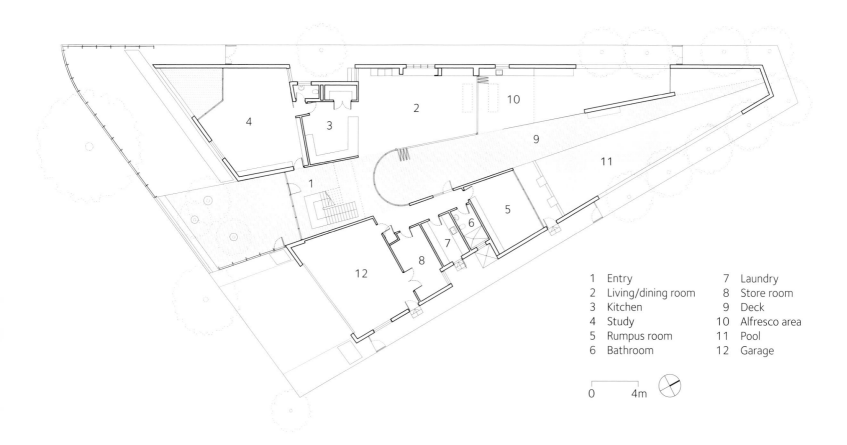

1 Entry
2 Living/dining room
3 Kitchen
4 Study
5 Rumpus room
6 Bathroom
7 Laundry
8 Store room
9 Deck
10 Alfresco area
11 Pool
12 Garage

0   4m

Courtyard House

New York, USA

Stelle Lomont Rouhani Architects

Located in the dunes of Amagansett, the existing courtyard house was well loved by its owners, but was in serious need of an upgrade. Systems were all outdated or inadequate, and the structure itself in poor shape. Since the owners did not want to part with the charm of the current configuration, but were in need of more bedrooms, Stelle Lomont Rouhani Architects sought a variance to rebuild the house, switching out some of the unusable two-storey height space for a second storey.

In keeping with the inside-outside theme, parts of the house are separated either horizontally or vertically by exterior spaces. A sun porch acts as a connector between main living space and bedrooms on the ground floor. This space completely opens up with folding doors in the summer time. An interior stair in the entry volume leads to the upstairs bedrooms, which are connected by a walkway with ample windows flanking both sides.

One of the main driving forces of the project was about keeping it green and keeping it simple. The house is designed to achieve lower maintenance and have less of a carbon footprint by employing evacuated solar thermal collector tubes to supply domestic hot water and radiant floor heating, photovoltaic solar panels to produce electricity and a green roof for lower heating/cooling loads. The structure itself is basic wood framing on cylindrical concrete footings. A mix of conventional products with inventive design are employed to keep cost down.

Photography by Matthew Carbone

1   Courtyard
2   Covered porch
3   Sun room
4   Kitchen
5   Dining room
6   Living room
7   Bedroom
8   Bathroom
9   Laundry
10 Powder room
11 Outdoor shower
12 Play room
13 Hallway
14 Deck

0   4m

Eastern
Influence

Sydney, Australia

Rolling Stone Landscapes

The client is a professional photographer with a downstairs studio and
the vista of the garden from his studio and the entertaining deck above
were of paramount importance. The client's desire to create a modern
Asian ambiance in his garden was achieved by incorporating Zen-
inspired architecture, materials and plants.

The area available for this project was at the rear of the property and called for a simplistic approach so that the theme could be felt without losing usability of the space. With this in mind, a black stone blade wall was installed with a circular steel vista window revealing a Japanese maple (Acer palmatum) and other soothing plant material behind it. The base of the wall is surrounded by a small pond with a basalt boulder placed within it – water falls onto the boulder from an outlet above. A hardwood deck was installed at the side of this water feature to provide a place to sit and experience the tranquil ambiance.

A lush green lawn works its way around the various structures, while maintaining straight lines to keep the space as generous as possible. Where small retaining walls were required, they were finished in a rendered texture and painted to complement the colour of the house. This colour also contrasts well with the installed stone paving.

Consisting of rectangular basalt tiles, the paving lends a dark tone to the layout. Hardwood timber inserts are also used – the same material used in the deck.

The planting of a themed garden is important in communicating a message. The slender weavers bamboo (Bambusa textilis 'Gracilis') used at the side boundary is perfect for the role of screen planting and best suits the theme. Also used were Japanese maple (Acer palmatum), little gem magnolia (Magnolia grandiflora 'Little Gem'), camellia (Camellia sasanqua), Japanese sago palm (Cycas revoluta), Japanese box (Buxus microphylla 'Japonica'), creeping juniper (Juniperus horizontalis), blue fescue grass (Festuca glauca) and mondo grass (Ophiopogon japonicus).

Photography by Danny Kildare

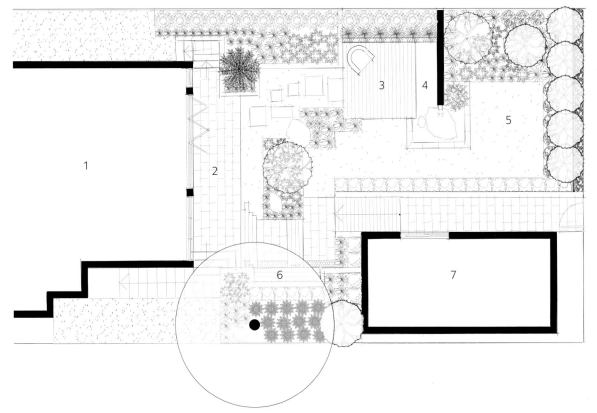

1   Existing residence
2   Paving
3   Timber deck
4   Water feature with water
    spout into pond
5   Lawn
6   Timber bench
7   Garage

Enclosed Open House

East Coast, Singapore

Wallflower Architecture + Design

The owners wanted a spacious, contemporary house that would be as open as possible without compromising security and privacy at the same time. Surrounded by neighbours on four sides, Wallflower Architecture + Design proposed a solution that included a fully fenced compound with a spatial programme that internalised spaces such as pools and gardens, which are normally regarded as external to the envelope of the house. By zoning spaces such as the bedrooms and servants' quarters on alternative levels, the ground plane was freed from walls that would have been required if public and private programmes were interlaced on the same plane. The see-through volumes allow a continuous, uninterrupted view from the entrance foyer and pool through the formal living area to the internal garden courtyard and formal dining area in the second volume. All these spaces are perceived to be within the built enclosure of the house.

The environmental transparencies at ground level and between courtyards are important in passively cooling the house. All the courtyards have been finished using different materials, creating temperature differences between the courtyards. This allows the living and dining areas and the pool house to become conduits for the breezes that move between the courtyard spaces. On the second floor, solid hardwood louvres that can be adjusted by hand allow the desired amount of breeze and sunlight to filter through.

For the owner, it is the experiential serenity of unencumbered space, a gentle breeze, dappled sunlight and the hush of water rippling on a pond that is priceless in the dense and busy urban landscape.

Photography by Albert Lim

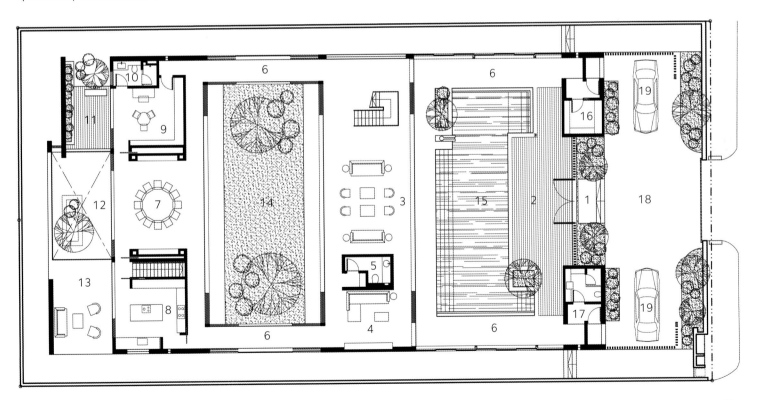

1	Entry	5	Powder room	9	Study	13	Outdoor terrace	17	Changing room
2	Foyer	6	Linkway	10	Bathroom	14	Courtyard	18	Driveway
3	Living	7	Dining	11	Outdoor deck	15	Pool	19	Carport
4	TV area	8	Kitchen	12	Void to basement	16	Store room		

0   4m

Hawthorn Residence

Melbourne, Australia

Steve Domoney Architecture

In purchasing this property the client sought the potential to restore and subdivide away the original Victorian dwelling, using the funds from this sale to develop a connected, yet quite individual residence for themselves on the remaining parcel of land.

Utilising the remaining Victorian outbuildings and working within the confines of an established garden with significant specimen trees to consider, a new residence emerged which now weaves its way around a central garden court, punctuated by the grandeur of the existing tree canopies. The new elements of the structure have been made light, skeletal and deliberately transparent so as to invite a dialogue between the new interior spaces and their garden setting. This experience is enhanced through the introduction of flowing lineal reflective ponds, which mark the transition from indoors to out and evoke a sense of tranquility throughout.

The lightness of structure helps ease the new residence into the garden without the sense of 'intrusion'. Its contrast with the fragments and solidity of the Victorian building is apparent. Here both are afforded a sense of being within the confines of the garden, side by side yet not crowding each other or striking discordant tones. Each appropriately represents the time in which they arrived at this place and both now seemingly content to co-exist within the garden setting.

Photography by Derek Swalwell

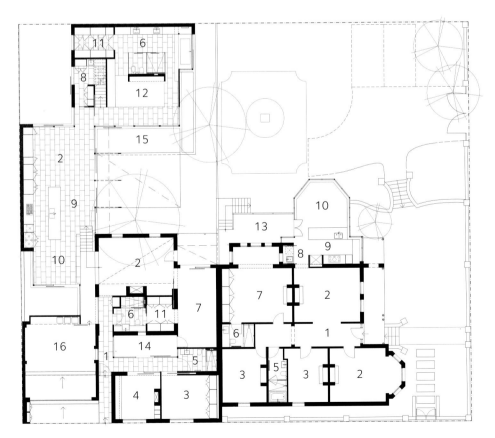

1   Entry
2   Living room
3   Bedroom
4   Study
5   Bathroom
6   Ensuite
7   Master bedroom
8   Laundry
9   Kitchen
10 Dining room
11 Dressing room
12 Sleeping pavilion
13 Deck
14 Courtyard
15 Pond
16 Garage

0   5m

JKC1

Singapore

ONG&ONG Pte Ltd

This is one of three 'good class bungalow' plots carved from a larger plot developed by the Keck Seng Group. The house sits on a slight incline and overlooks a pool in the front yard, following the feng shui belief of balancing the 'mountain' and 'water' elements.

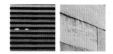

The first floor living and dining area is a vast and continuous space, providing an unobstructed view of the pool and front lawn. The generously proportioned kitchen with laundry area is located at the back of the house together with the garage.

A centralised combination staircase leads up into the open courtyard, which is directly above the kitchen. The master suite with bedroom, walk-in wardrobe and bathroom are all to the left, while the children's bedrooms and adjoining playroom occupy the opposite side. In the middle, a multi-purpose family area takes up the front section,

while the back area houses an additional room. From the courtyard, a spiral staircase ascends onto the terrace that can serve as a barbecue or entertainment area where guests can take in the beautiful views of the surrounding greenery.

This house is distinguished from the surrounding residences by its generous use of space, making it a welcome relief from Singapore's high-density urban environment.

Photography by Derek Swalwell

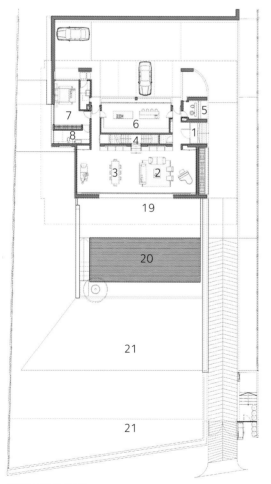

GROUND FLOOR

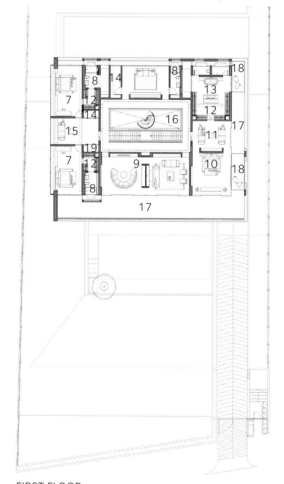

FIRST FLOOR

1 Entry
2 Living
3 Dining
4 Staircase
5 Powder room
6 Kitchen
7 Bedroom
8 Bathroom
9 Family room
10 Master bedroom
11 Master bedroom foyer
12 Walk-in wardrobe
13 Master bathroom
14 Storage
15 Hall
16 Courtyard
17 Balcony
18 Water feature
19 Timber deck
20 Pool
21 Garden

0   5m

Kooyong Residence

Melbourne, Australia

Matt Gibson Architecture + Design

The brief for the renovation of this Gold Rush-era double-fronted Victorian home originally called for full demolition. However, there was potential in retaining the front section and the client was encouraged to restore it.

The new double-storey addition is separated from the old (two 'pavilions') by a glazed prism that traverses the open courtyard area, acting as a passive temperature regulator and a powerful interstitial space mediating the two buildings and history. The journey from the front door through the main axis to the rear of the site sets up a series of 'delayed thresholds', and highlights the separation of the pavilions.

The rear addition is reconfigured around solar access and greater flexibility and connection to the position of the sun. The use of radial-sawn timber cladding (internally and externally) encourages a more sculptural and playful point of difference to the rigidity and masculinity of the existing building.

This project puts forward a case that for sites of this size, 'continuity' and 'newness' together, but separated, may in fact be a more respectful, robust and sustainable outcome. It utilises and exploits the juxtaposition to heighten and delight in the difference whilst following adaptive methods that encourage retention and re-use over demolition.

Photography by Shannon McGrath

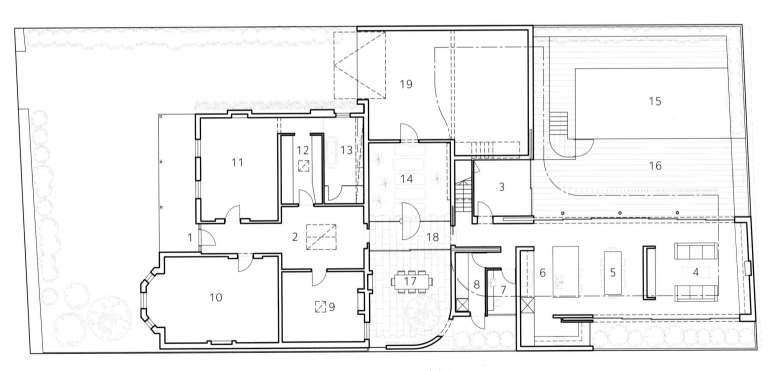

1	Formal entry	6	Kitchen	11	Master bedroom	16	External dining area
2	Vestibule	7	Powder room	12	Walk-in robe	17	Sheltered sun court
3	Snug	8	Laundry	13	Ensuite	18	Prism
4	Family room	9	Guest bedroom	14	Informal entry	19	Double garage
5	Dining	10	Drawing room	15	Pool		

0   3m

Leichhardt House

Sydney, Australia

Rolf Ockert Design

The site is located in a heritage conservation area that is fiercely protected by the local government. In consultation with planning officials, Rolf Ockert Design proposed maintaining and preserving the existing house in its entirety while designing a visibly modern two-storey addition.

To avoid the addition overlooking any of the neighbouring sites, the design included high-level slot windows to the side laneway, thus allowing tree and sky views while maintaining privacy. These slots then became a major design feature that was then continued in the pattern on the side façade.

As the site was very narrow, the internal layout of the building had to be organised very simply. The linear stairs are not placed in line with the existing corridor of the old house but on the other side of the extension. As a result the relatively small space reads to be quite generous.

To facilitate ease of construction whilst maintaining integrity of the original building, the existing house was kept completely intact and largely untouched. A glass side strip and rooflights were inserted between the old and the new, not only clearly defining the two but also bringing light into the core of the house.

The architects worked with Alex Noyce from Art of Nature to design the courtyard. As a result of good communication between all parties and great sensitivity to the architectural design, the landscape design marries to the overall concept beautifully. The large kitchen and dining area opens up directly to the courtyard, which works to create a sense of space despite the restricted available space.

Photography by Paul Gosney

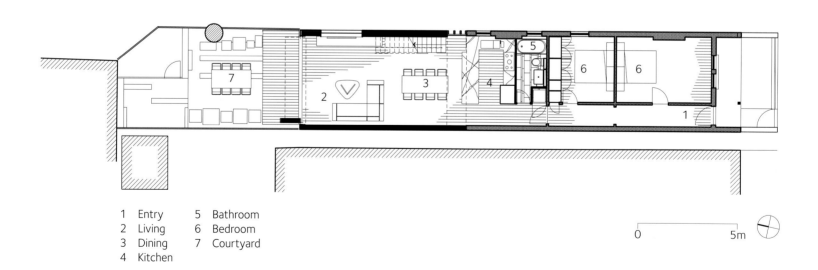

1 Entry
2 Living
3 Dining
4 Kitchen
5 Bathroom
6 Bedroom
7 Courtyard

0   5m

Marimekko House

Perth, Australia

Ariane Prevost Architect

Marimekko House is a creation of its place and of its inhabitants. A synthesis of art, sculpture and architecture, it is a simple, budget-driven dwelling for five adults designed for the common rituals of daily family life. A defining character of the house is derived from its simplicity, functionality and material alchemy of combined textures of natural, raw and recycled and industrial materials selected for their beauty, economics and low maintenance.

Defined by a site-specific context, the planning, detail and construction are combined with an ecological, sustainable approach and intended to last through time and be low-impact. The raised and sloping topography of the site, located between a parkland and cul-de-sac, gives rise to the dynamic floor plan – a dexterous arrangement of public space and private retreats that interact to configure the U-shaped dwelling around a central northern courtyard, one of a number of principal alfresco areas over two main levels that provide a very distinct way of living indoor and out, every day for every season.

A theatrical architectural statement in the form of a Marimekko Joonas patterned Corten steel brise-soleil façade combines with a weeping hanging garden inviting the visitor on an intriguing journey through a secret side-gate to an oversized pivot-door to the centre of the house, dramatically showcasing the lush interior through a long moving glass wall dividing the flowing seamless bricked floor throughout the whole level.

The clandestine rooftop garden offers an exclusive private 'under the stars' living and sleeping space and lush garden experience (with vegetables, trees and a gazebo) for passive surveillance over the urban context while maintaining visual and audible contact with the lower-level courtyard through a skylight and various open-aspect balcony screens.

A raised cantilevered concrete platform and timber-lined loggia with cook's fireplace offers verdant parkland views at the rear of the house and provides cosy, roll-down screens for winter fireside outdoor living.

The whole of the house may be opened to engage in uninterrupted circular access between the different alfresco spaces via inside and outside stairways providing for whole of site use with the house as an open pavilion.

Photography by Bo Wong

1   Entry
2   Study
3   Bedroom
4   Northern courtyard
5   Kitchen
6   Scullery/laundry/pantry
7   Dining
8   Living room
9   Terrace
10 Master bedroom
11 Master bathroom
12 Office
13 Roof deck
14 Roof garden

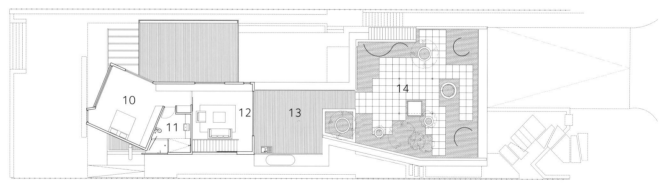

FIRST FLOOR

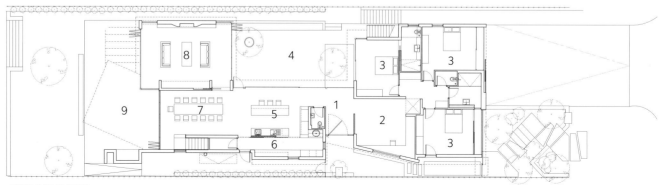

0   5m

GROUND FLOOR

Mary
Residence

Melbourne, Australia

Matt Gibson Architecture + Design

This Victorian terrace renovation celebrates old and new whilst
marrying periods with differing connections of interior and exterior.
Rather than 'two stylistic pavilions' this 367-square-metre
(3,950-square-foot) home is instead an orchestrated combined
whole connected through simultaneous differentiation and
consistency in material, colour and detail.

The rear is intended as a contemporary interpretation of the front – a strongly designated functional program yet with progressive spatial 'editing out' (selective removal of walls breaking down the Victorian interior containment). A central light court extends to become a pivotal feature providing a powerful interstitial space. Full-height glazing here and at rear enables a breezeway and temperature regulator, offering users the flexibility to change the seasonal formation of the dwelling.

Allocations of surface, threshold and junction are rigorously explored – the existing dwelling retains its high Victorian grandeur, the lowered volume contains a relaxed, contemporary, comfort-driven approach.

Colour is utilised in a unifying gesture – darks and lights are utilised in combination with naturally finished materials throughout the entirety of the home with an intended limitation and consistency so as not to compete with the interaction with the exterior.

The project questions and encourages an architecture concerned with historical 'story-telling' celebrating both 'continuity' and 'newness'.

Photography by Shannon McGrath

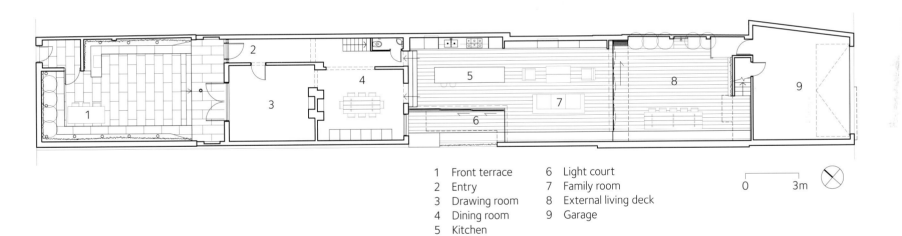

1 Front terrace
2 Entry
3 Drawing room
4 Dining room
5 Kitchen
6 Light court
7 Family room
8 External living deck
9 Garage

0   3m

Meera Sky Garden House

Sentosa Island, Singapore

Guz Architects

The Meera Sky Garden House has been designed with a central void and largely shallow volumes, particularly on the upper floors, which maximise cross ventilation and reduce dependence on mechanical air conditioning.

The large shaded areas of glazing on most rooms reduce the reliance on artificial lighting during daylight hours while minimising solar gain and the large acrylic window in the basement level media room floods it with diffused natural light, further reducing energy consumption. The gardens on each level typically overhang the storey below, providing shade and reducing overheating in Singapore's tropical climate.

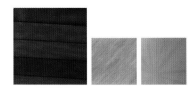

The concept of the Meera Sky Garden House is strongly influenced by the ambition of enhancing the occupants' quality of life. This is largely achieved by the roof gardens on every level. As well as having direct access to these, interior spaces have large areas of glazing with views out over the gardens to the sea and sky. The large amount of natural daylight brought in contributes strongly to a good indoor environment. Large acrylic windows in the pool result in even the basement receiving great amounts of diffused natural light.

The design of the open air stairwell cutting through the centre of the building reduces the depth of indoor areas and encourages cross ventilation. Using the natural cross ventilation to its potential, along with the assistance of mechanical ventilation when necessary, produces a high indoor air quality important to the wellness of inhabitants.

The house's integration with nature and the outdoors is most evident in the garden areas on every level. The gardens, with much planting and a number of trees, reduce carbon dioxide and help counter greenhouse gas emissions. The large areas of grass absorb much less heat than conventional roofing materials resulting in less thermal storage in the building itself, reducing the required use of cooling systems.

In the tropical climate of Singapore, with heavy rainfall, water retention of garden areas will also contribute to reducing the pressure on the surface water system at peak times.

Photography by Patrick Bingham-Hall

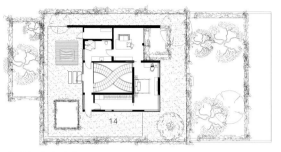

SECOND FLOOR

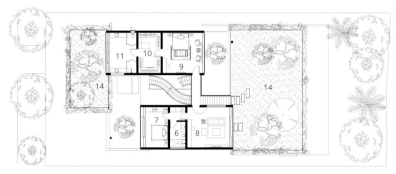

FIRST FLOOR

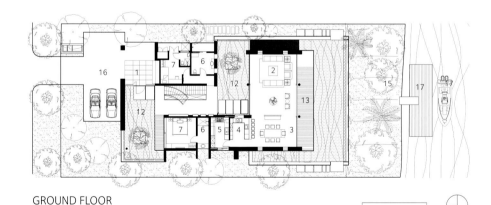

GROUND FLOOR

0   5m

1 Entry	7 Guest bedroom	13 Deck
2 Living	8 Family room	14 Roof garden
3 Dining	9 Master bedroom	15 Garden
4 Dry kitchen	10 Master closet	16 Carport
5 Wet kitchen	11 Master bathroom	17 Jetty
6 Guest bathroom	12 Fish pond	

North Fitzroy House

Melbourne, Australia

NMBW Architecture Studio

By adding a courtyard garden to this substantial existing house between the house and the new kitchen and living addition, NMBW Architecture Studio managed to retain the solidity but not noticeably increase the volume of the original building. This courtyard space also allows for a new entry to the house from the more quiet side street, creating a quieter, more relaxed feeling immediately.

Contained by the main house, the courtyard space and the addition are slightly rotated towards the north and a new fence. The original house can be seen from across the courtyard and the addition is low, extending to the back of the property to become part of the fence on the southwest corner. The fence, the building and the sliding shade screens are clad in the same dark stained vertical timber with the containment of garden space and built space being treated with equal importance.

The courtyard is generous, giving more vegetation to the street. The inside spaces of the addition interact through the courtyard space over the courtyard fence to the row of houses opposite and the park space beyond. This is a dynamic relationship as steps up in the floor level

change the extent that you can see depending on where you are and what you are doing. The small study space has a vantage point looking into the courtyard and back to the old house when seated and then over the fence to the park, the train and the distant rise when standing.

The courtyard vegetation is a strong presence from the kitchen and living room. Within the kitchen and living space views shift between close and intimate views into the courtyard and distant views beyond. It suits different moods – times to be separate and others to be engaged.

Photography by Peter Bennetts
Planting by Amanda Oliver

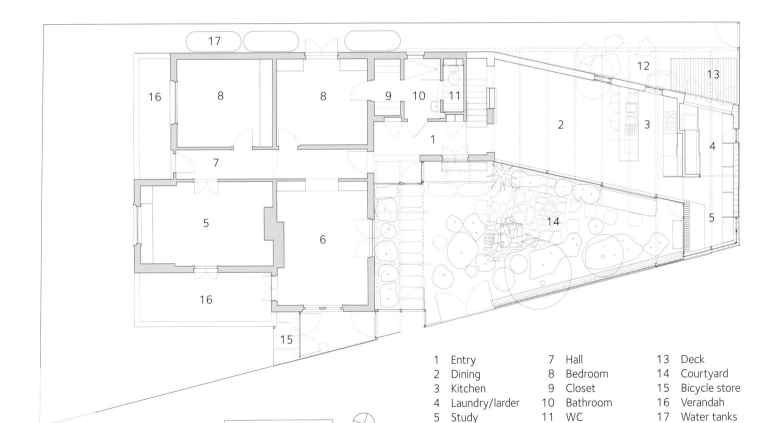

1 Entry
2 Dining
3 Kitchen
4 Laundry/larder
5 Study
6 Living room
7 Hall
8 Bedroom
9 Closet
10 Bathroom
11 WC
12 Kitchen garden
13 Deck
14 Courtyard
15 Bicycle store
16 Verandah
17 Water tanks

0   5m

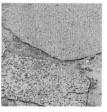

Oriole Way Residence

Los Angeles, USA

McClean Design

At the end of Oriole Way overlooking Sunset Strip, this lot was more of a cliff than a site but it featured one of the best views in the city. The challenge faced by McClean Design was to graft the 743-square-metre (8,000-square-foot) house onto the hillside and create a suitable entry experience and enough living space despite the steep topography. They achieved this by separating the garage and parking area from the entry of the house, which took advantage of the street slope and allowed pedestrians to enter at the main level of the home while giving the architects the opportunity to create a water- and light-filled entry courtyard.

Laid out over three levels, the house takes advantage of the slope to separate the bedrooms from the main living areas. The lower level comprises bedrooms, a large dedicated theatre, a gym and a wine room. The main level consists of the entry, living, dining and kitchen spaces as well as the master bedroom. The four-sided infinity-edged pool along with the timber deck brings the city view into the house and allows for a fantastic entertaining area. The upper level features a loft space, an additional bedroom and a roof terrace to highlight the magnificent views available.

The two-storey living room is a rarity in the neighbourhood and coupled with light coming from all sides gives the house an expansive feel. With a black and white palette, the house is sleek Hollywood, and makes plenty of use of marble, dark granite and chrome as well as high gloss cabinets and custom wallpaper.

Photography by Nick Springett

FIRST FLOOR

GROUND FLOOR

1 Entry
2 Living room
3 Family room
4 Kitchen
5 Laundry
6 Dining room
7 Powder room
8 Master bedroom
9 Master bathroom
10 Master closet
11 Guest bedroom
12 Guest bathroom
13 Guest closet
14 Catwalk
15 Entry courtyard
16 Patio/deck
17 Pool and spa
18 Overlook
19 Rooftop terrace
20 Pool
21 Garage

0   3m

Otago Courtyard House

Lake Hawea, New Zealand

Glamuzina Paterson Architects

The Otago Courtyard House is grounded in rural land at the foot of Mount Maude in the Otago region in New Zealand. The driving force behind the formal arrangement of the house was the physical context and thus the house became an enquiry into where a site begins and ends – questioning the definition of boundary and the way that landscape may be inhabited. Firmly dug into the earth, its low form and simple square plan recall the modest language of early settler buildings in the region. Responding formally to the immediate context within which it is placed, the idea of a singular form clad with simple materials drove the exploration of design.

In their written brief the clients requested 'a building not built on a domestic scale, that might have been part of a larger assembly that sits on the ground with weight and permanence'. The couple planned to retire to the house and spaces were tailored to their respective hobbies by unusual titles, such as the quiet room and the music room. The 250-square-metre (2,690-square-foot) house had a strict construction budget, which needed to be adhered to closely.

Clad in brick amour, the façade addresses continuous enclosure, framing view to the lofty mountains and low plains. The plan was able to negotiate both the interior courtyard and the exterior landscape. Living, dining and sleeping spaces occupy the northern and eastern edges, favouring the predominant direction of the sun, while niches and overhangs in the building envelope protect it from the hot, dry summers and harsh winters. The use of rusticated bricks creates a material relationship with the site and anchors it firmly to the ground, along with a textural palette that allows for a constantly shifting interpretation of scale. Shifting roof planes and concrete floor plates enable the house to articulate the relationship of form to land. This in turn is mediated by a plinth, expressed as a low recessed wall wrapping around the building connecting the mass to the ground and acting as an organisational tool for apertures.

Photography by Samuel Hartnett

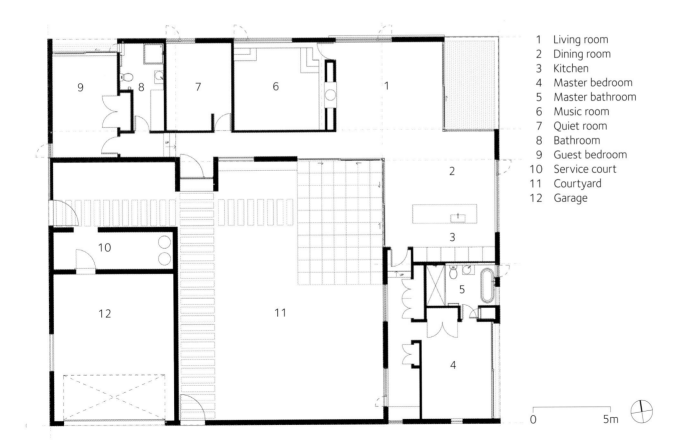

1 Living room
2 Dining room
3 Kitchen
4 Master bedroom
5 Master bathroom
6 Music room
7 Quiet room
8 Bathroom
9 Guest bedroom
10 Service court
11 Courtyard
12 Garage

0   5m

Rising Glen Residence

Los Angeles, USA

Janna Levenstein/Tocha Project

This residence is grounded in true formal characteristics, which are offset by expressive geometric imbalances that stimulate unpredictability. Strong sight lines were formed by setting walls, floors and ceilings to draw away and toward each other in unison. Greenery was cultivated into the home's spaces and planted to enliven the floors and walls of bath areas. To encourage circulation, water features and pathways glide throughout the home. At the entry, a path of original 1950s terrazzo leads from outside to inside and around the main body of the home to adjacent rooms that branch off from the path.

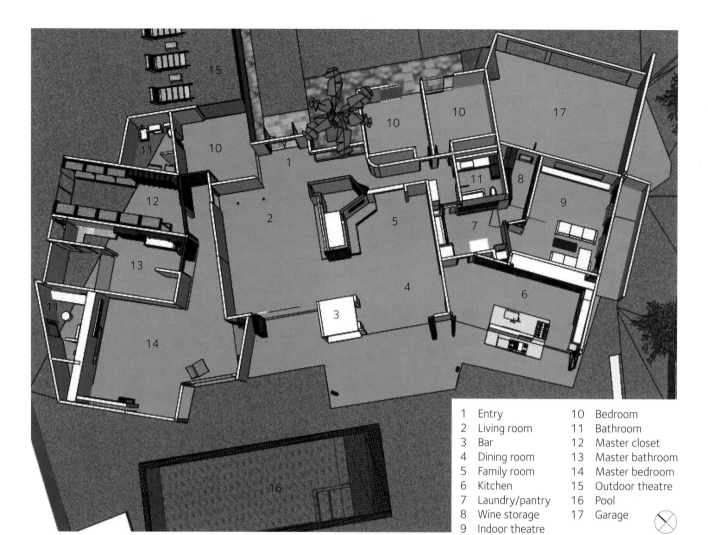

1	Entry	10	Bedroom
2	Living room	11	Bathroom
3	Bar	12	Master closet
4	Dining room	13	Master bathroom
5	Family room	14	Master bedroom
6	Kitchen	15	Outdoor theatre
7	Laundry/pantry	16	Pool
8	Wine storage	17	Garage
9	Indoor theatre		

The kitchen hosts a massive monolithic island of poured polyurethane that radiates from inside to the outside cooking area. The bar features a hinged oversized window that gracefully tucks to the side, permeating the outdoor space.

Carefully customised thin profile bi-fold doors reflect the inside and outside environments. A variety of exotic woods are used for cabinetry, wall veneers and sinks to add warmth and balance against the pristine doors. These warm wood tones, along with rich, muted colour tones, amplify the spaciousness and elegance of the space while fuelling a contrasting rhythm of bold and subtle in the modern habitat.

Photography by Michael McCreary and Katarina Malmström

Robinson House

Auckland, New Zealand

Dorrington Architects & Associates

This much-loved family home with sweeping views warranted a sensitive renovation that acknowledged the original placement and layout. An extensive renovation project ensued and included a new pool and associated pool house and courtyard, landscaping, and the re-cladding and roofing of the existing building.

The main house features black-stained board and batten gabled 'sheds' in homage to the rural setting. Internally the house was completely re-planned and finished, giving more appropriate priority to the size and layout of the individual spaces.

The original footprint of the house remained untouched, with the new pool area situated to the west of the house, flowing seamlessly from the living room and guest wing. Tiling throughout the house continues outside as paving, creating an uninterrupted connection from the main house to the pool area.

The pool pavilion is designed as a roof plane sitting lightly on a stone landscape wall at one end and an oversized steel frame at the other. The stone wall steps and continues around the pool area, containing the space.

The pavilion can be entirely opened up or protected from the prevailing wind via glass sliders. A bar and fireplace allow for entertaining adjacent to the main structure.

A reflection pond to the north of the house, viewed from the kitchen and main living area, further enhances the feel of light and airiness that plays throughout this home, contrasting with the solid, black cedar timber cladding.

Photography by Emma-Jane Hetherington

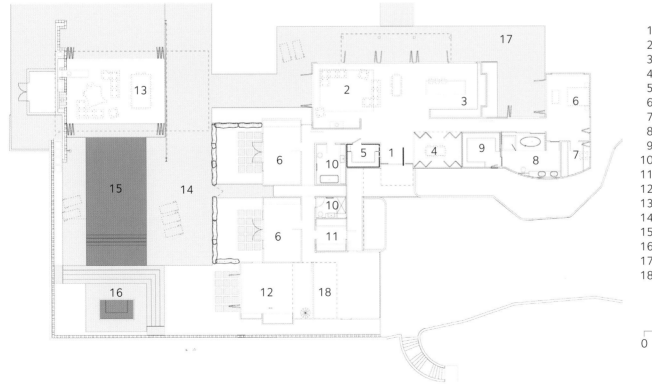

1   Entry
2   Lounge
3   Kitchen
4   Dining room
5   Cellar
6   Bedroom
7   Study
8   Ensuite
9   Dressing room
10   Bathroom
11   Laundry
12   Media room
13   Pool room
14   Courtyard
15   Pool
16   Spa
17   Reflecting pond
18   Garage

0   3m

Rooftop Garden

New York City, USA

Rebecca Cole GROWs

Landscape designer Rebecca Cole designed this rooftop garden atop an historic 110-year-old landmark building in Manhattan's Upper West Side for a client who travels extensively through the year and wanted a space where he could relax and feel as if he was on holiday. Despite building code and spacial challenges, the result is a flexible and private rooftop space amid the hustle and bustle of the city.

With a view of the water tower and building turret at one end of the outdoor living space a repetition of tall Miscanthus grass helps to balance and 'ground' the design to the roof. The round sofa sectional softens the hard angles of the building's edge while mimicking the round turret and water tower.

As local building codes did not permit the entire roof to be clad in wood, play tiles were used to create a soft play area for the children. Birch and maple trees are interspersed with linear groupings of lower perennials lining the entire edge of the area, providing flexible and safe use while still allowing city views to stand out.

With the rustic wood and low resin chairs creating a comfortable space and flexible seating furniture, the space has a kind of loft feeling with an open concept with multiple areas for dining, relaxing and entertaining.

Photography by Jarrard Cole

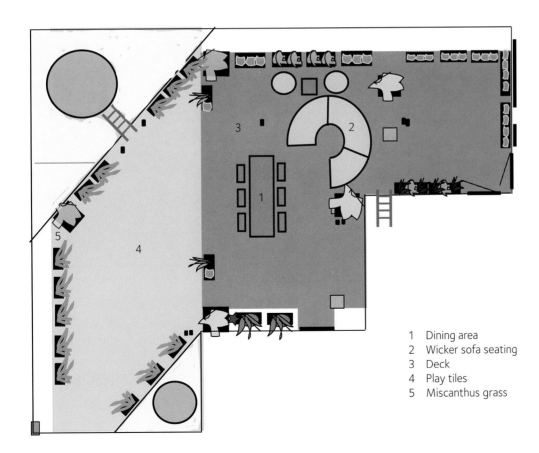

1   Dining area
2   Wicker sofa seating
3   Deck
4   Play tiles
5   Miscanthus grass

SGNW House

Zimbali Coastal Resort, South Africa

Metropole Architects

Zimbali Coastal Resort is situated in lush sub-tropical coastal forest on the KwaZulu-Natal North Coast, and overlooks miles of pristine deserted beaches, and the warm Indian Ocean. Zimbali – 'The Valley of Flowers' in Zulu – is richly endowed with the beauty of abundant indigenous fauna and flora including over 200 species of birds, Bushbuck, Blue Duiker, Vervet monkeys and Banded Mongoose. The architecture within Zimbali Coastal Resort is harmonious with nature, and encompasses elements of the Tropical Asian Vernacular theme.

Significantly influenced by traditional Japanese architecture, as well as Frank Lloyd Wright's masterpiece, Fallingwater, SGNW house harmonises with its natural context. The large overhanging roof forms and cantilevers, including the main suite which cantilevers 6 metres (20 feet) over the outside entertainment area below, combined with the glazed ground floor, represent and continue the coastal forest tree canopy.

Large amounts of glazing optimise views of the indigenous bush that encapsulates the house, and together with the palette of raw materials, including natural timber, grey travertine cladding, water and natural stone cladding, dissolve the separation between inside and outside.

Water is a primary component in SGNW House. Several bodies of water, including Koi ponds, water features and a rimflow swimming pool appear to coalesce into one, and flow through the house and

out into the forest. There are two waterfall level drops in the swimming pool, which provide the evocative sound of water falling throughout the ground floor living spaces. The house is entered over water with a timber bridge spanning the Koi pond into the double volume entrance hall, which is itself an island surrounded by glass panels through which the Koi pond is viewed. The Koi can alternatively be viewed through a glazed slot in the floor of the kitchen, as the pond is linked with a tunnel under the house, through which the fish can traverse.

SGNW house is a sensually rich experience, with its palette of carefully considered natural finishes, sound of falling water, connection with nature including vistas of indigenous forest, fresh breezes and bird call, which all transport the resident to an experiential paradise of peace and tranquilty and a sense of well-being.

Photography by Grant Pitcher Photography

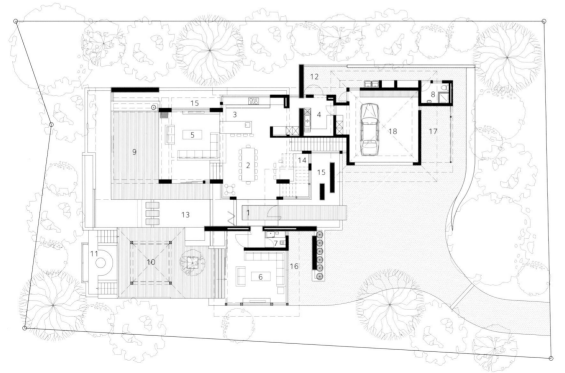

1   Entry
2   Dining room
3   Kitchen
4   Scullery
5   Family room
6   Private lounge
7   Powder room
8   Change room
9   Covered patio
10 Covered pergola
11 Boma
12 Yard
13 Pool
14 Water feature
15 Koi pond
16 Golf cart parking
17 Covered carport
18 Double garage

0   3m

Skycatcher House

Atsugi, Japan

Kazuhiko Kishimoto/acaa

Skycatcher House is built right in the middle of typical suburb residential quarters found throughout in Japan. Surrounded by a mixture of single and double storey buildings, the house features a courtyard in the middle of the building, which works to facilitate a sense of privacy, and has a simple square outer appearance. Most windows face the courtyard rather than the outside, creating a private yet brightly sunlit environment.

In having the entrance open directly onto a courtyard, architect Kazuhiko Kishimoto from acaa has created an environment that allows the client to feel relaxed from their first step. Another focus of the courtyard design is the sense of depth. The courtyard takes a complicated planar form due to walls and glass panels separating indoor and outdoor spaces. Every wall and glass panel facing the courtyard is aligned at a degree other than horizontal or vertical. This creates a sense of flow into the courtyard and, along with the open roof design, helps create such depth that it is easy to forget that this is all one house within the confines of an ordinary residential block.

The indoor passageway surrounds the courtyard to achieve the longest possible flow within the confines of the space. The bedrooms and living rooms face a verandah, which also serves as the only access to these rooms. Inspired by traditional Japanese houses, this outdoor verandah-cum-corridor provides residents with a chance to appreciate their own private landscape throughout the year.

Photography by Hiroshi Ueda

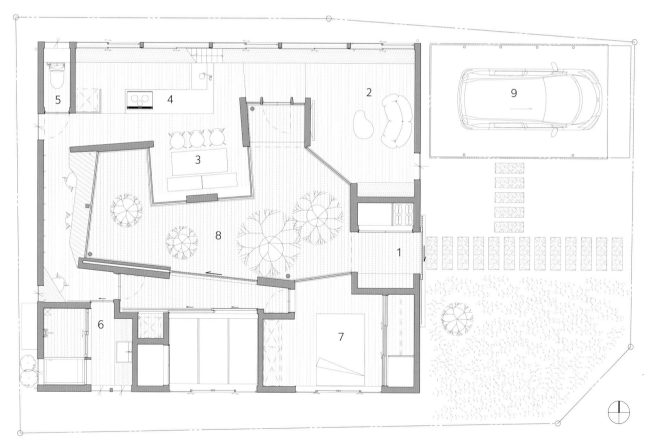

1   Entry
2   Living room
3   Dining
4   Kitchen
5   Powder room
6   Bathroom
7   Bedroom
8   Courtyard
9   Garage

Smith
Residence

Cremorne, Australia

David Boyle Architect

Architect David Boyle updated this Federation-style house within a heritage conservation area with the addition of a contemporary single-storey structure and open-plan living area. The project involved the demolition of unsympathetic additions and offered new living spaces at the rear of the house opening directly to the rear yard and to a new eastern courtyard created between the new pavilion and the existing house.

The new pavilion steps up from the existing house to mediate the natural ground levels, and has been sculpted to respond to a mature jacaranda tree in the rear yard. The kitchen opens to both the rear yard and the central covered courtyard space. Bathrooms and skylights have been added within the existing structure and extend the existing hall into an informal sitting room opening east to the central covered deck. The roof of the deck is raised above the pavilion roof to allow northern light into the courtyard and includes a kick back roof parallel to the existing tiled roof to allow western light to be filtered between the two roof planes. Additionally, the choice of materials provided a contemporary texture compatible with the decorative Federation features of the house.

The project explored the relationship of house and garden to maximise the sense of space and the opportunity for the interplay of an appropriate level of natural light to provide an open yet protected suburban environment.

Photography by Brigid Arnott

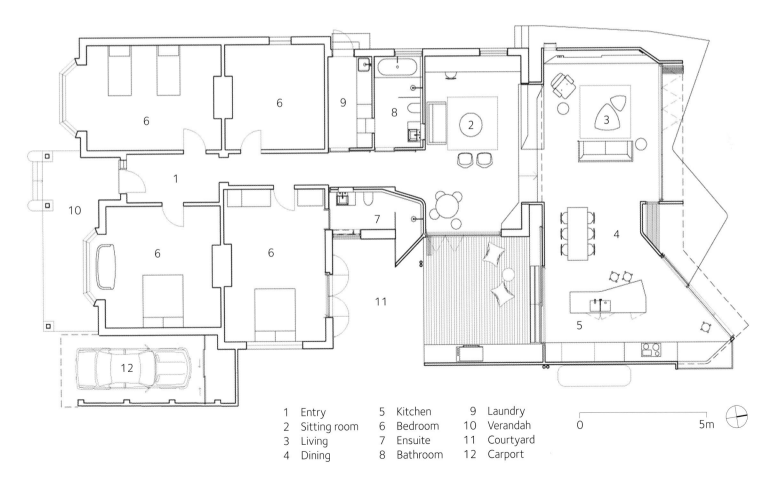

1 Entry	5 Kitchen	9 Laundry	
2 Sitting room	6 Bedroom	10 Verandah	
3 Living	7 Ensuite	11 Courtyard	
4 Dining	8 Bathroom	12 Carport	

0   5m

Storrs Road Residence

Sunshine Coast, Australia

Tim Stewart Architects

This 18-hectare (44-acre) site has had a life that has ebbed and flowed with the life of the family who have owned it for almost 30 years. Developed from the ground up into a small orchard by a growing family, the farm is now retreating back to its natural form as the owners also wind down in retirement. The original home was subdivided and sold many years ago whilst the family pursued a different chapter of their lives and the opportunity for a new home presented a chance to reflect the clients' changing values and lifestyle.

With the clients' field of reference reducing with age, the home aims to reflect in miniature the site as a whole and its history. Located on the site of the original water tanks that supplied irrigation to the orchard and water to the first home, the house is now the new epicentre of the property. The new home is entered across a large dam-fed pond to the outdoor room, which takes in the striking views that are a feature of the site. The rest of the house then wraps around a courtyard garden and the same interests that once led to the development of an orchard now tender a garden, which, whilst decorative, can easily surprise with random appearances of tomatoes, herbs and other vegetables.

All the elements of the home engage with both the garden and the view. As the elements of the original property make their way closer to the house, more and more food-providing plants are becoming an integral part of the garden, reflecting the clients' more self-sufficient lifestyle. The home itself is far more environmentally conscious than its predecessor, with low-energy lighting a predominant feature and solar water heating with over 60,000 litres (15,850 gallons) of water storage. Built with timber taken from the site and from fire breaks cut through the bushland, the timber was also milled and finished onsite and makes up all of the exposed timber as well as the flooring and much of the sub-structure.

Photography by Christopher Frederick Jones

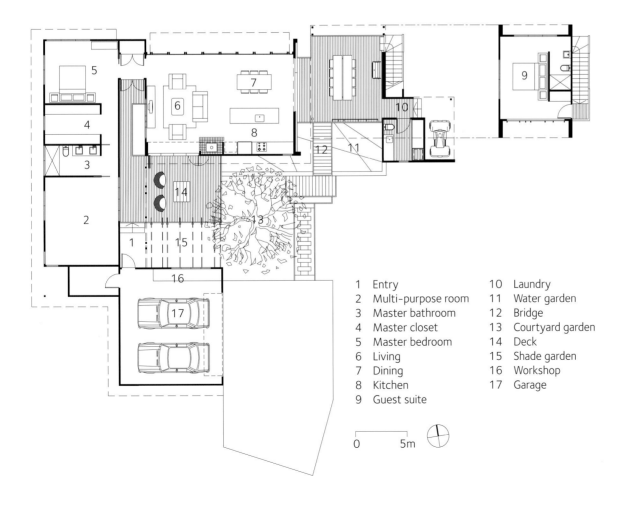

1   Entry
2   Multi-purpose room
3   Master bathroom
4   Master closet
5   Master bedroom
6   Living
7   Dining
8   Kitchen
9   Guest suite
10 Laundry
11 Water garden
12 Bridge
13 Courtyard garden
14 Deck
15 Shade garden
16 Workshop
17 Garage

0   5m

Story Pool Pavilion

Texas, USA

Lake | Flato Architects

Having designed the Story Ranch a number of years ago, Lake | Flato Architects was commissioned to design a 'sunrise to sunset' outdoor family gathering place – the last piece in the puzzle for this private home.

Set apart from the more private ranch house, the land comprises a series of plateaus with expansive views to the Texas Hill Country. One plateau had served as an informal gathering spot for years, with a lonely, restored Airstream trailer and firepit, so it was here that the architects placed the new structure.

The simple, open-air, steel and wood 'outdoor living room' pavilion has two thick Texas limestone 'boxes' that house a full working kitchen behind folding slatted wood doors, a screened bath area and storage. The Airstream was given its own special environment with a small private deck under a vine-covered arbour structure, all nestled in the shade of a large grouping of trees. At night, the wood deck patio is illuminated by track lighting, creating an evening space to suit any lifestyle. With the addition of the swimming pool, perfect for cooling off from the Texas sun, this much-loved oasis is complete.

Photography by Casey Dunn and Brent Humphreys

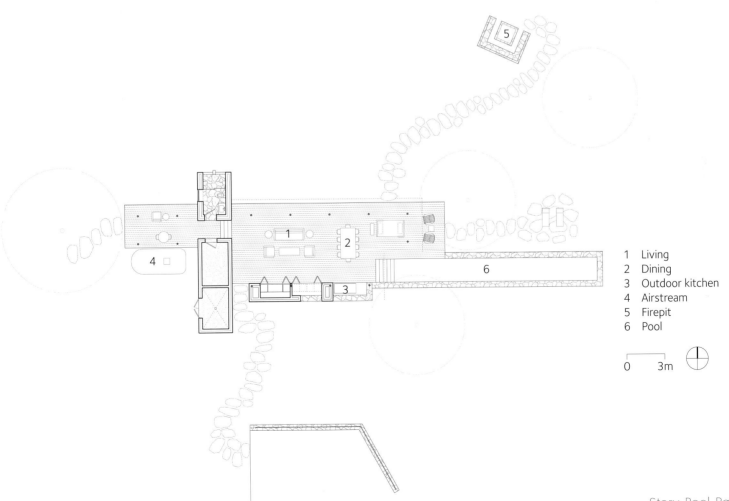

1 Living
2 Dining
3 Outdoor kitchen
4 Airstream
5 Firepit
6 Pool

0   3m

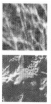

Sunken
Connections

Sydney, Australia

Rolling Stone Landscapes

This garden was showing its age and not relevant to the new owners of this property. Dean Herald of Rolling Stone Landscapes was called upon to review how best to update the space to cater for the entertaining they did for their friends and family. The design work was not limited to the external areas but also included the internal space, along with doors and windows.

Rolling Stone Landscapes began to explore the possibilities of creating dedicated external spaces for each entertainment activity. With the existing pool level set, they saw the opportunity to use a change in levels to help communicate the different areas. With this in mind, a sunken lounge area was created with fixed hardwood bench seating dressed with soft cushions. A Japanese box hedge (*Buxus microphylla* var. *japonica*) surrounds the seating along with a custom-made stainless steel ice box for convenient storage of drinks. Also within this space is a raised stone wall with a wood fireplace, a timber storage display and a planter box above that softens the structure.

Adjacent to and above this space is a functional outdoor kitchen with all the necessary appliances for entertaining, including a double glass-door refrigerator, a teppanyaki barbecue, a sink and generous bench space for the preparation of meals. This area is covered with a flat roof structure with heaters, making it a usable space during the colder months of the year. The dining area is positioned on a raised

deck to give it definition from the large bluestone pavers installed throughout the other areas. The table was designed and fabricated to best suit this location and included an Eco fire in the centre of the area, which creates a great atmosphere in the evening. New retaining walls give shape to the garden and surround the pool while preserving the existing plant assets, such as a rather large mature date palm.

Japanese sago palms (*Cycas revoluta*) were added to the existing plant material, along with little gem magnolias (*Magnolia grandiflora* 'Little Gem'), slender weavers bamboo (*Bambusa textilis* 'Gracilis'), xanadu (*Philodendron* 'Xanadu') variegated mondo (*Ophiopogon intermedians* 'Stripey White') and star jasmine (*Trachelospermum jasminoides*). To maximise views of this new outdoor living space, new frameless glass doors were installed at the rear of the home along with a new kitchen layout and adjoining living and dining area.

Photography by Danny Kildare

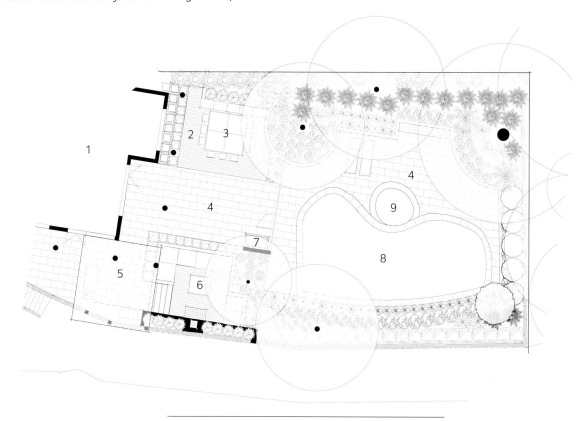

1 Existing residence
2 Timber deck
3 Dining area
4 Paving
5 Outdoor kitchen
6 Sunken lounge with fireplace
7 Outdoor shower
8 Pool
9 Spa

Tanager Residence

Los Angeles, USA

McClean Design

Tanager Way is one of the most popular streets in the Hollywood Hills and this lot is located on the west side, where it is possible to pick up sweeping views of the city and Beverly Hills all the way to the ocean beyond. With this 740-square-meter (8,000-square-foot) home, McClean Design's primary objective was to maximise the views from the main living spaces and the master bedroom.

This was achieved by pushing the bedroom out over the pool and moving the body of the house forward, creating a courtyard in front to allow additional light into the home. The courtyard contains an attractive water feature with a vertical water wall, allowing for privacy from the street. The primary rooms are located on the entry level with a family room and entertainment areas below as well as additional bedrooms.

A unique feature of the home is the media room on the lower level which was conceived as a wooden box within the family room that could open to the remainder or the space to provide a more casual movie watching environment or close off within itself. The palette of the home is bright contemporary with large floor slabs of white stone, high gloss cabinets and different varieties of marble.

Photography by Nick Springett

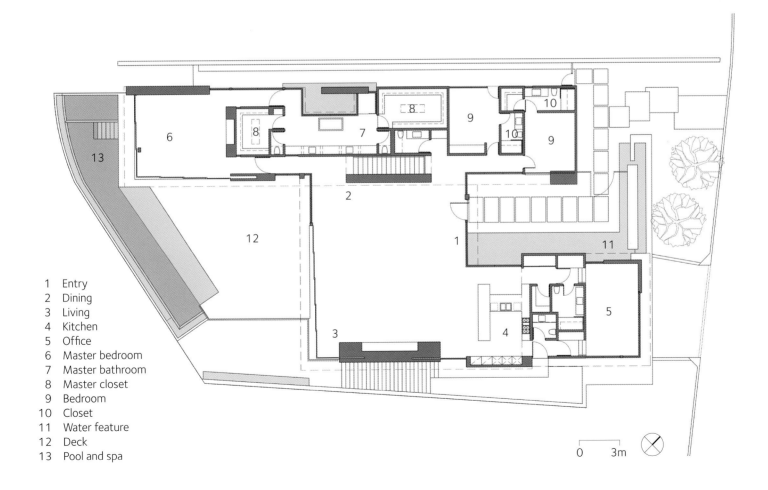

1 Entry
2 Dining
3 Living
4 Kitchen
5 Office
6 Master bedroom
7 Master bathroom
8 Master closet
9 Bedroom
10 Closet
11 Water feature
12 Deck
13 Pool and spa

0   3m

The Six

Arizona, USA

Ibarra Rosano Design Architects

The Six is a project comprised of six courtyard houses that demonstrates the possibilities for higher density, urban infill desert development that is respectful of its time and place.

In keeping with the character of the adjacent historic house and the tradition of courtyard houses in the region, Ibarra Rosano Design Architects sited the houses to include large central courtyards hidden behind plaster walls. The monastic quality of the elevation creates mystery and surprise, reminiscent of Tucson's historic adobe rowhouses.

The central courtyard is traditionally employed in hot, arid regions because it takes advantage of cool desert nights by affording the house the ability to open into a secure and private space. Here, Integra® insulated block walls exploit both thermal mass and high insulation to passively regulate the interior temperature.

The primary focus of the main living space is its connection to the central courtyard. Directly above the expansive kitchen island, the ceiling rises dramatically in height to provide a transition from the cooking area, and allows clerestory windows to provide balanced south and north light for the voluminous dining and living area. The glue-laminated wood beam window seat overlooks the

courtyard and visually and functionally extends the space in the gallery hall that accesses the bedrooms and garage. The master bedroom shares access to the central courtyard while the master bath as well as the guest bath look onto small private courtyards, offering privacy, light and connection to the exterior.

While the Six takes cues from Tucson's architectural past and the neighbouring historic adobe house – the central courtyard, plastered masonry walls and minimal western exposure – it is an emphatic expression of our time and place in future history.

Photography by Bill Timmerman

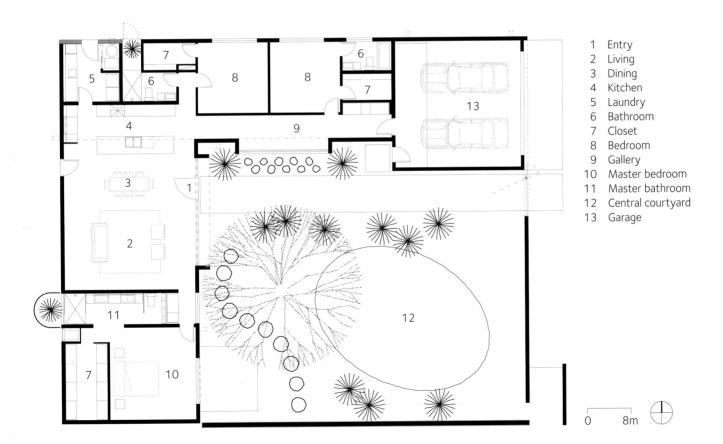

1 Entry
2 Living
3 Dining
4 Kitchen
5 Laundry
6 Bathroom
7 Closet
8 Bedroom
9 Gallery
10 Master bedroom
11 Master bathroom
12 Central courtyard
13 Garage

0   8m

Under Pohutukawa

Piha North, New Zealand

Herbst Architects

For this beach-side home in New Zealand, Herbst Architects were presented with an extremely challenging site. As part of a continuous belt of forest that edges the road along the beach front, more than 90 per cent of the site is covered in mature pohutukawa trees. As such, the circumstances not so much allowed, but dictated a sensitive poetic response to a building that, in order to exist, would require the destruction of a large number of mature trees.

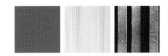

Separating the brief loosely into private and 'public' components left the project with smaller individual masses with which to articulate the forms. The private functions of bedrooms and garage are housed in two towers, which are construed as freshly sawn stumps of the trees that were removed. To allude to the bark of the stumps, the skins of the towers are clad in black/brown stained rough sawn irregular battens. The interior spaces are then seen as carved out of the freshly cut wood, achieved by detailing all the wall, ceiling and cabinetry elements in the same light timber.

The public space connects the two towers and attempts to engage with the surrounding pohutukawa forest by defining a crossover space between the powerful natural environment and the built form. The plane of the roof form pins off the towers to engage with the continuous tree canopy, disintegrating from a rigid plane to a frayed edge which filters light in a similar way to the leaf canopy. The primary structure holding up the roof is a series of tree elements, alluding to the trunks and branches of trees but detailed in a rigorous geometric arrangement. This suggests an ordering of nature as it enters and forms the building.

The height of the public space with its light glass division responds to the height of the surrounding trees. The roof plane is partially glass to allow the full extent of the trees to be felt as they lean over the building. A walkway links the towers at the upper level allowing engagement with both the natural and man-made canopies.

Photography by Patrick Reynolds

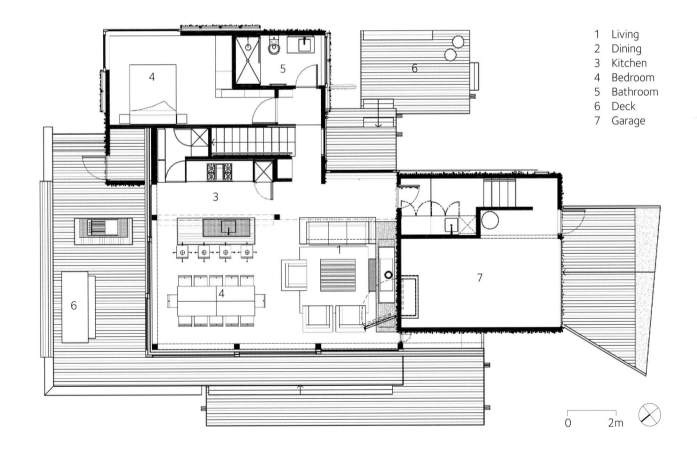

1 Living
2 Dining
3 Kitchen
4 Bedroom
5 Bathroom
6 Deck
7 Garage

0   2m

Victoria Avenue Residence

Auckland, New Zealand

Architektur Ltd

Behind the austere busy street frontage on Victoria Avenue lies a generously proportioned family home, designed primarily for entertaining. With five double bedrooms, eight bathrooms, four living areas, a state-of-the-art kitchen and three-car garaging, it sits on a fantastic site in one of New Zealand's premier suburbs.

The 1,244-square-metre (13,390-square-foot) site is long in the east-west direction, giving it great natural daylight and passive solar gain. The house was designed to step down the site away from the road towards the west, where the primary living areas are located. This allows for an superb outdoor seating and barbecue area under the 200-year-old native Pohutukawa tree, which helps filter the sometimes-harsh New Zealand sun.

Set over three levels, the long sleek lines of this house belie the massive 780 square metres (8,395 square feet) of internal floor area. In addition, a small poolhouse and tranquil pool and spa are located at the western end of the property. The driplines of two significant trees to be retained dictated the separation of the poolhouse from the main house.

The ground floor is dedicated to the four living areas and the generous kitchen, and the five double bedrooms, complete with ensuite bathrooms, can be found on the first floor. With the basement featuring a home theatre, games room, gymnasium, 1,000-bottle wine cellar, laundry and plant rooms, this house caters for every conceivable activity and comfort.

The entire western end of the first floor has been dedicated to the master bedroom suite, which, with its large roof deck, looks out over and through the canopy of gracious ancient native trees.

Photography by Jim Janse

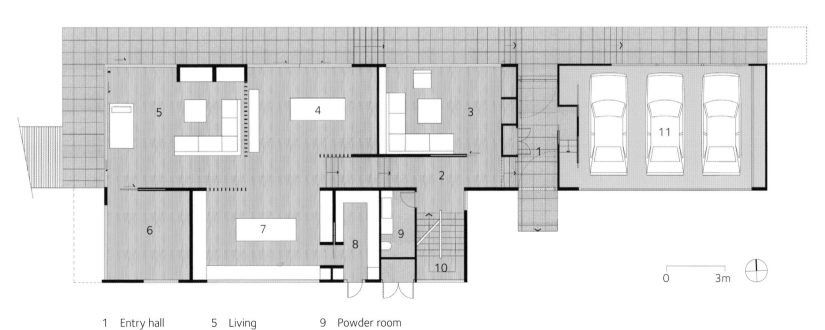

1	Entry hall	5	Living
2	Hall	6	Formal dining
3	Lounge	7	Kitchen
4	Informal dining	8	Scullery
9	Powder room		
10	Stairwell		
11	Garage		

Villa del Cielo

Nevada, USA

Paddle Creek Design

A Lake Las Vegas jewel, Villa del Cielo offers all the finest amenities of new construction while capturing the timeless charm and Old World ambience of a European village. A main 606-square-metre (6,524-square-foot) two-storey villa plus four private and beautifully appointed casitas look as if they've taken centuries to perfect. Three casitas serve guests and the fourth functions as a private office and library. The air-conditioned garage houses three vehicles and a separate golf cart port is also provided. Guests can take in the sunsets from the salt-water pool and waterfall spa.

Perfectly placed to frame panoramic views of Lake Las Vegas, Rainbow Mountain and Montelago Village, Villa del Cielo represents the finest of Lake Las Vegas offerings. Owner and designer, Lori Venners of LVI Design, envisioned a home that lived and looked old – warm, comfortable and inviting. Teamed with Texas architect Thomas Oppelt of Paddle Creek Design and builder Greg Kaffka, the vision came to life. The project spanned four years from the initial project meetings to completion. The compound boasts an incredible attention to detail and features authentic and reclaimed materials from Europe, Ecuador and Mexico. The driveway is historic reclaimed sandstone cobblestone from Western Europe. The Spanish roof is two-piece clay tile imported from Spain and installed with a blend of colours to establish an authentic look of moss and natural stains. The hardwood flooring uses a combination of reclaimed and hand-scraped Austrian ash, larch and spruce and other reclaimed materials include cabinetry, beams, fireplace materials and terra cotta flooring imported from Southern France. The exterior and dining room canterra stone was hand quarried and imported from Tlaquepaque, Mexico. Custom carvings and hand-painted murals add an artistic touch of elegance.

Integration of the latest technology makes this Old World home modern and energy-efficient. The lighting system is automated and there is a state-of-the-art sound system throughout, including rock speakers hidden in the landscape. The home incorporates a steam shower, dry sauna, security cameras, automated exterior lighting, halogen cabinetry lighting and a 13-zone heating and air conditioning system. Most window and French doors are dual pane argon gas filled glass with silver oxide coating. Twenty-first century conveniences meet pure Old World luxury in this one-of-a-kind home.

Images courtesy of Gene Northup of Synergy Sotheby's International Realty

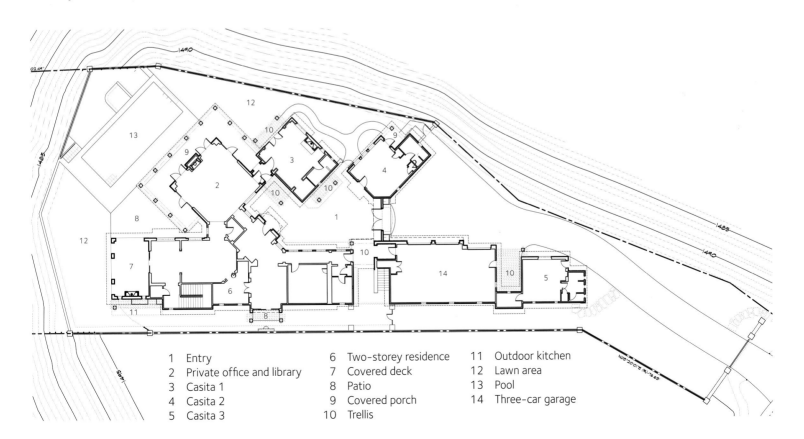

1 Entry	6 Two-storey residence	11 Outdoor kitchen
2 Private office and library	7 Covered deck	12 Lawn area
3 Casita 1	8 Patio	13 Pool
4 Casita 2	9 Covered porch	14 Three-car garage
5 Casita 3	10 Trellis	

Index of Architects

The information and illustrations in this publication have been prepared and supplied by the author. While all reasonable efforts have been made to source the required information and ensure accuracy, the publishers do not, under any circumstances, accept responsibility for errors, omissions, and representations express or implied.